T0006211

Who Was Amelia Earhart?

by Kate Boehm Jerome

illustrated by David Cain

Penguin Workshop

With love to another fearless aviator—
my husband, Robert Jerome—KBJ

For Laighton Hall Cain—
whose imagination soars—DC

PENGUIN WORKSHOP
An Imprint of Penguin Random House LLC, New York

Visit us online at www.penguinrandomhouse.com.

Library of Congress Control Number: 2002007760

ISBN 9780448428567

60 59 58

Contents

Who Was
Amelia Earhart?

Amelia Earhart was a pioneer. This doesn't mean she traveled west in a covered wagon or lived in a log cabin. It means she had a special spirit. She liked to be the first to do new things.

In the 1920s, Amelia became a pilot. This was in a time when the airplane was still a new invention. Not many people

knew how to fly one. It was even more unusual for a woman to fly planes. But Amelia set many flying records to prove that she was the best.

Amelia helped start the airline business in the United States. She also was a writer, a speaker, and a fashion designer. But it all started from her love of flying.

Amelia was a pioneer in another way, too. She thought that women deserved to have the same rights as men. This was at a time when women were fighting for the right to vote. Many people still thought women were not strong enough or smart enough to have jobs outside the house. But Amelia's actions proved that bravery and brains were not for males only.

Unfortunately, Amelia did not live to see old age. Just before her fortieth birthday, she tried to set a new record. She wanted to be the first woman to fly all the way around the world. But Amelia and her plane went down somewhere in the Pacific Ocean. She was never seen again.

Most people remember Amelia Earhart for the last event of her life. But this is a story about everything that came first.

Chapter 1
Young Amelia

Amelia Mary Earhart was born in her grand-mother's house in Atchison, Kansas, on July 24, 1897. The house was high on a hill. It had eleven rooms. Maids and a cook worked there. Dinner was served on fine china.

Amelia's mother's parents had a lot of money. But Amelia's father had trouble keeping a job. Edwin Earhart could barely make the payments on the family house in Kansas City. There were always

money worries. But Amelia loved her parents—especially her handsome, funny father.

When Amelia was seven, her father had enough money to take the family to see the World's Fair in St. Louis, Missouri.

Twenty million people came to the 1904 World's Fair. Forty-five countries set up exhibits.

WORLD'S FAIRS

World's Fairs have been popular events throughout the history of United States. In 1876, a Centennial Exposition was held in Philadelphia. It marked the one hundredth anniversary of the signing of the Declaration of Independence. Ten years in the making, this World's Fair introduced people to many new things. One of the most popular exhibits showed a "new" machine called the typewriter!

In 1893, a fair called the World's Columbian Exposition was held in Chicago. It was a grand event. One area at this fair was called the Midway Plaisance. The Midway featured popular entertainment. Here, the first Ferris wheel was introduced. It stood 260 feet tall and had 36 cars. It could hold more than two thousand people when full!

"Building the World of Tomorrow" was the motto of the World's Fair held in New York City in 1939. A popular exhibit at this Fair was the Futurama. Visitors sat in moving chairs to get a glimpse of a city in the future. Modern buildings and huge highway systems "wowed" people of all ages. Another exhibit also got a lot of attention. Here people stared at a new invention called the television. Many wondered what good it might be in the future!

St. Louis World's Fair, 1904

At the St. Louis Fair there were Eskimo villages and Japanese gardens. Each nation and state showed something about its own culture.

Amelia and her younger sister, Muriel, saw a big roller coaster at the fair. When she got back to

Kansas City, Amelia tried to build one in her yard.

Muriel, Amelia's uncle, and another friend helped. Wooden tracks ran from the top of a shed to the yard below. A little buggy rolled down the

tracks. The tracks were greased with fat to make the buggy go faster.

Always the bravest kid on the block, Amelia was the first to try out the roller coaster. She dragged the buggy up to the top of the tracks and got on. Her sister held her feet. When Amelia gave the signal, Muriel let go. Amelia went down head-first . . . and crashed!

Did this stop Amelia? Not at all. She and her friends made the slope of the tracks less steep. Then she got on the buggy again. This time she

made a good run. She loved the speed. And it was almost as if she were flying through the air!

On a cold day in December, Amelia went sledding with her sister. Amelia wanted to go very fast. She took a running start. Then she jumped on the sled, lying head first on her stomach. The hill was icy. Amelia was gaining speed. Suddenly, there was trouble below. A horse-drawn wagon came out from a side street. It was directly in Amelia's path. And Amelia couldn't stop.

At the last second, Amelia ducked. She and her sled slid right under the horse. A moment later Amelia was up and smiling. Her quick thinking had helped her avoid a bad accident.

In the summer before eighth grade, Amelia went to another fair. The Iowa State Fair. Here, Amelia saw her first airplane.

BROTHERS IN FLIGHT

Orville Wright
1871–1948

Wilbur Wright
1867–1912

Orville and Wilbur Wright never went to college, but they were good at building things. On December 17, 1903, in Kitty Hawk, North Carolina, they made history. That was the day their airplane, the Wright Flyer, went one hundred feet in the air.

The Flyer was a rickety plane by today's standards. Its body was made of cloth stretched over a wood frame. It had one small engine and two propellers. Many thought it would crash on takeoff. But it didn't. The Flyer stayed in the air 12 seconds. A short trip indeed, but this first flight changed history forever.

It was 1909—only six years after Wilbur and Orville Wright had made their famous flight at Kitty Hawk, North Carolina. Surprisingly, Amelia did not think too much of the airplane. She was always adventurous, but her love of flying came much later.

Amelia's teenage years were hard. Her father couldn't keep a job, and the family split up. Amelia's mother took the girls to Chicago. They lived in a rooming house and Amelia went to Hyde Park High School.

Amelia was a good student. She dreamed of going to a first-rate college. But there wasn't enough money. However, Amelia's mother was able to send her to a good private school for girls.

It was time for Amelia to start out on her own.

Chapter 2
A Woman of Character

In the fall of 1916, when Amelia was nineteen years old, she boarded a train for the Ogontz School in Pennsylvania. Amelia didn't mind going far away from home. She was starting on a new adventure.

The head of the Ogontz School was a woman named Miss Sutherland. At first, Amelia did not like her. But in time, she changed her mind. Miss Sutherland was strict but very smart. She had opinions on

all sorts of subjects. And although Miss Sutherland had had many chances to marry, she never did. Miss Sutherland was more interested in her career than a husband. Miss Sutherland was an independent woman

who made a big impression on her pupils.

The other students and teachers at Ogontz admired Amelia. She was shy but

charming. She was a good athlete. She was also a practical girl. In a letter home to her mother, Amelia wrote, "I don't need spring clothes so don't worry about sending me money . . . I know you all need things more than I." Once Amelia even bought hand-me-down shoes from a friend.

In her second year, Amelia was elected vice-president of her class. Amelia wrote the class motto. She strongly believed in what it said.

"Honor is the foundation of courage."

While Amelia was at Ogontz, the United States entered the First World War. During the Christmas holidays of 1917, Amelia went to Toronto, Canada. Her sister Muriel was in school there. Amelia's mother also joined them.

In Toronto, Amelia saw soldiers who had been

wounded in the war. Amelia wanted to help. Within a week, she made a decision: she was not going back to Ogontz. Instead, she would stay in Toronto. Amelia would train to be a nurse's aide and work in a hospital. People who knew Amelia weren't surprised. Amelia always acted on what she believed in.

WORLD WAR I

It was called the Great War . . . but it was really terrible. More than 30 million people were wounded or died in World War I between the years of 1914 and 1918. At the beginning, only Germany and Austria-Hungary were fighting against the allied forces of Britain, France and Russia. As the war dragged on, more countries got involved. The United States joined the Allies, entering the War in April 1917.

By the summer of 1918, about 200,000 American soldiers were being sent to Europe each month.

These soldiers often lived in deep ditches. They dug these trenches for protection as they fought. It was called "trench warfare."

Peace finally came with an Allied victory in November of 1918. Most people thought there could never be another war like this. Unfortunately, they were wrong. Only twenty years later the world exploded into World War II.

Chapter 3
Amelia Chooses a Career

Amelia worked in a Toronto hospital until World War I was over. Then she came back to the United States. She wanted to study science. Maybe she would become a doctor. Amelia decided to enroll at Columbia University in New York City.

At that time, most men wanted wives who would stay at home. That was fine

with most women. But not Amelia. She could not understand why a woman had to give up work just because of a wedding ring.

Amelia wanted a career—she just couldn't decide *what* career she wanted. After

WOMEN'S SUFFRAGE MOVEMENT

Sounds painful, doesn't it? But the word "suffrage" doesn't mean "suffering"–it's about getting the right to vote.

It wasn't until the 1890s that Wyoming became the first state to let women vote. By 1913–when Amelia Earhart was a high school student–women could vote in only 12 of 48 states. But the voices of protest were getting louder. "Suffragettes" marched in the streets. Many were arrested and put in jail. But the fight continued. Finally, on August 26, 1920, the Nineteenth Amendment of the U.S. Constitution was passed. Women in every state of the union had won the right to vote.

some time at Columbia, Amelia quit school again. She went to Los Angeles. Amelia's parents were back together again, and she moved in with them. Amelia's family was hoping that Amelia would settle down soon.

Amelia was seeing a young man named Sam Chapman. Sam asked Amelia to marry him. But Amelia knew that Sam would not want her to have

a career. She said no. Amelia knew what she didn't want. Still, she was drifting.

Then, on Christmas Day in 1920, her life changed. Twenty-three-year-old Amelia Earhart and her father were with a crowd of people in Long Beach, California. They were all looking up into the sky. Why? An air show was taking place.

Pilots raced each other in their planes. They also did incredible tricks like wing walking.

Amelia was fascinated. She had just one question. How much would it cost to take flying lessons?

At that time, there were no airports or runways. Planes took off from big, empty fields. Three days later, Amelia and her dad went to Rogers Field. It was there that she took her first plane ride.

The flight was ten minutes long. The pilot sat in front. Amelia sat behind him. The cockpit was completely open. Amelia and the pilot wore goggles to protect their eyes.

The plane bounced across the bumpy field for takeoff. Then it slowly rose into the air. Right away Amelia was hooked. She later said "As soon as we left the ground, I knew I, myself, had to fly."

Amelia was not drifting any longer. From that day on, she had a goal. Amelia was going to become a pilot.

At nearby Kinner Airfield, a woman named Neta Snook gave flying lessons. A woman pilot—

this was just what Amelia wanted. Neta agreed to teach Amelia to fly. It would cost $1.00 a minute. In 1921 that was a lot of money—but Amelia was willing to pay.

The next day Amelia arrived for her first flying lesson in riding pants, boots, and a jacket. She had walked three miles from the streetcar to the airfield. But she wasn't tired. She was excited that her dream was about to come true.

That first day, Amelia only taxied the plane on the ground. But it wasn't long before she was up in the air. Amelia was a good student. She just seemed to know naturally what to do.

Neta and Amelia became good friends. At twenty-four, Neta was only one year older than Amelia. Amelia wanted to learn all about airplanes. She pestered Neta with questions all the time.

When the weather was good, Amelia practiced flying. When the weather was bad, Amelia didn't waste that time. She read and studied about flying.

Amelia also learned to repair airplanes. She cut her long hair short. She bought a leather jacket.

The jacket was soon wrinkled and oil-stained. Amelia didn't care. Learning about airplanes kept her busy all the time.

Soon Amelia wanted her own plane. With her mother's help, Amelia bought a small one at

Kinner Airfield. Neta thought the plane was too small to be safe. Amelia ignored her. She had her plane painted yellow, and she named it the *Canary.*

On December 15, 1921, Amelia took the test for her license. It was a little less than one year

from when she took her first lesson—but she passed.

Amelia Earhart was now an airplane pilot.

Chapter 4
Amelia Takes Off

With her pilot's license in hand, Amelia flew in some air shows. Most pilots were men, so a young woman attracted a lot of attention. Amelia didn't like to be on display. But she worked in the shows to earn money. She had to keep on flying.

Then Amelia's friend and teacher, Neta Snook, got married. Just as Amelia feared, her friend's flying days were over. Neta would now be a wife and mother. So Amelia needed another instructor. She teamed up with an expert named Monte Montijo. Monte had flown in the army. He also did stunt work flying in the movies.

Monte taught Amelia a lot. She even learned to do tricks in the air like huge upside-down loops.

Now she felt like trying for a flying record. Amelia wanted to see how high she could go.

Amelia didn't tell anyone her plans. She had an instrument put in her plane. It measured how high above ground the plane was. In the early 1920s, planes didn't fly as high as they do today. One reason was because the cockpits were open. At higher altitudes there is not much oxygen to breathe. Amelia knew she could

pass out if she went too high. But she
was willing to risk it.

It took two attempts. Amelia flew through fog and sleet. She finally made it to fourteen thousand feet—more than two and a half miles high. Then her plane's engine began to fail. Amelia brought her plane down fast. She was just barely able to make a safe landing. But she had her record.

Although Amelia loved to fly, she soon found out that she couldn't support herself just by flying. There were no big airlines or airplanes yet. People did not travel by plane. In fact, most people never expected to take a ride in a plane. In 1924, Amelia temporarily gave up on her dream. She sold the *Canary* and used the money to buy a car.

You might guess that Amelia would pick a practical automobile like the Ford Model T. She

didn't. She bought a fancy yellow convertible. If she couldn't fly in the air, she would at least have the feeling of flying across the ground. Amelia named her car the *Yellow Peril*. She and her mother drove across country and headed for the East Coast.

Amelia went back to Columbia University. But again, it wasn't for long. She had to drop out again; as usual, the problem was money.

Sam Chapman followed Amelia out East. He proposed marriage again. It was tempting. Amelia was now 28 years old. Most people thought women this age were already "old maids." If Amelia married Sam, she wouldn't have to worry so much about money. However, Sam would want her to stay at home and have children. Amelia had to decide.

To her, the choice was very clear. Amelia told her sister Muriel of her decision. "I don't want to marry him," Amelia said. "I don't want to marry anyone." Amelia couldn't stand the thought of giving up her freedom.

The next job Amelia found was in Boston. She worked at Denison House where she took care of

poor children. Amelia really liked the job. She knew she was doing something worthwhile.

Flying was now limited to weekends. But she watched other pilots with interest. In 1927, a man named Charles Lindbergh made news all over the world. He was the first pilot to fly alone across the Atlantic Ocean. It took him more than 33 hours to fly from Long Island, New York, to Paris.

A woman from London named Amy Guest wanted to be the first woman to fly across the Atlantic. Guest was not a pilot so she would set the record just by being a passenger in the plane. George Putnam, a book publisher in New

George Putnam

York, was going to oversee her attempt. However, Amy's family wouldn't let her go. So George Putnam had to find another woman—and this time, he wanted a pilot.

CHARLES LINDBERGH—AVIATION HERO

Charles Lindbergh started out as a barnstormer. That's what pilots who did daring tricks at early air shows in the 1920s were called. But on May 21, 1927, Charles left his tricks behind and entered the record books. No one had ever made a solo trip across the Atlantic before. It was very dangerous; his plane, called the Spirit of

St. Louis, was only 28 feet long. Lindbergh's biggest problem was staying awake, so he'd stick his head out of the plane's window for blasts of cold air. He also kept reminding himself that if he slept, he would die.

Putnam ran a big publishing company so he knew a lot of people. He was good at making deals. Putnam asked a friend to find the right woman for the trip.

The friend found Amelia Earhart.

Chapter 5
Amelia Becomes a Hero

Amelia met with both George Putnam and Amy Guest in New York. They both thought she was perfect. Attractive. Polite. Well-educated. She got the job.

The job was actually not nearly as good as it sounded. Amelia wouldn't get paid. A man named Wilmer Stultz would fly the plane. He'd get twenty thousand dollars. And although Amelia was called "the captain," she was really just a passenger.

Why did Amelia agree? First, no woman had ever crossed the Atlantic by plane. The experience alone was enough to make Amelia go. Amelia summed up her feelings in a letter to a friend. "When a great adventure's offered you—you don't refuse it, that's all." Amelia also hoped that, if the trip were successful, all the attention could bring her other flying jobs.

The flight was very dangerous. Charles Lindbergh had made the trip safely. But fourteen

other people had died trying to cross the ocean. Three had been women. Still, two other women pilots were already planning to try it. Amelia had to move quickly if she wanted to be the first.

The plane, called the *Friendship*, took off from Boston on June 3, 1928. However, the crew had to land in Canada because of bad weather. Many days went by. The *Friendship* was still not able to take off.

Amelia discovered another problem. Her pilot,

Wilmer Stultz, drank too much. If Wilmer got drunk, she knew he couldn't fly the plane. But if they did not take off soon, Amelia would lose the record. It was now or never.

On June 16, Amelia made a decision. She told Wilmer to get ready to fly—they were leaving the next day no matter what. On the morning of June 17 Amelia sent a cable to George Putnam back in Boston. The cable read "Violet. Cheerio! A.E." Violet was a code word. It meant that the *Friendship* was taking off.

WESTERN UNION

Received at Western Union Building Boston

CABLE, CANADA

1928 JUN 17 AM

GEORGE PUTNAM

VIOLET. CHEERIO!

A.E.

Through the long flight Wilmer Stultz and his co-pilot "Slim" Gordon took turns flying the plane. Amelia wrote notes in her journal. After twenty hours of flying, they knew they were low on fuel. Could they find land in time?

The answer was yes. The *Friendship* touched

Route of the Friendship

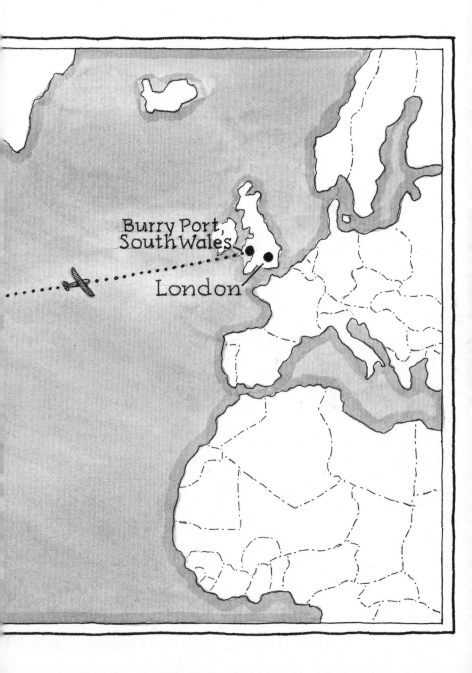

down in Burry Port, South Wales, twenty hours and forty minutes after taking off from the Canadian coast. They had done it. On June 18, 1928, Amelia Earhart became the first woman to fly across the Atlantic Ocean.

What came next was a surprise for Amelia. The

trip made her an instant hero. Amelia hadn't flown the plane. But people still thought she was very brave.

In London, Amelia was entertained by the rich and famous. She had tea with royalty.

On her return to America, Amelia was met

with even greater excitement. There were parades and speeches. Crowds of people wanted to see and hear the brave female. Many people compared Amelia Earhart to the famous pilot, Charles Lindbergh. They thought that Amelia, who was tall and slim, even looked like Lindbergh. Amelia's nickname became "Lady Lindy." George Putnam liked this a lot. He knew he could make Amelia even more famous.

All the attention was hard on Amelia. Sometimes she was frightened by the push of people trying to get near her. However, Amelia was a smart woman. She knew she would have to be in the spotlight if she wanted to fly planes and break records. Amelia also knew that if people got excited about flying, then the tiny airline business would grow. Amelia hoped to be a part of that business.

If Amelia made speeches, she would also be paid. That meant that she could buy another airplane. With her own plane she could set more records. That would lead to more speeches—and more money. For the first time in her life, Amelia started to believe that she could actually make a living by flying.

George Putnam became Amelia's manager. He set up lots of public appearances for her. In six months Amelia made over one hundred speeches and gave more than two hundred interviews.

Amelia did not complain about her busy schedule. She was given a new car for an appearance at an auto show. She also made money by letting companies use her name to advertise their products. The fur-lined, leather "Amelia Earhart Flying Suit" became very popular in a New York department store. Amelia also became an editor for *Cosmopolitan* magazine and wrote a column about aviation. Amelia didn't really like to write, but the articles brought more publicity. Many of the magazine's readers thought that Amelia was a good role model for young girls.

By 1929, Amelia was the best-known female pilot in America. But what Amelia really wanted was more time flying. So a week before she turned thirty-two, Amelia purchased a secondhand Lockheed Vega. It was a big plane that was hard to handle. But it was built for speed and distance. As soon as possible, Amelia wanted to set more records.

The first women's cross-country air race was going to be held later that summer. It was called the Women's Air Derby. Whoever flew from Santa Monica, California, to Cleveland, Ohio, in the shortest time would win. Amelia was eager to enter.

The course, which went over the Rocky Mountains, was dangerous. The rules committee

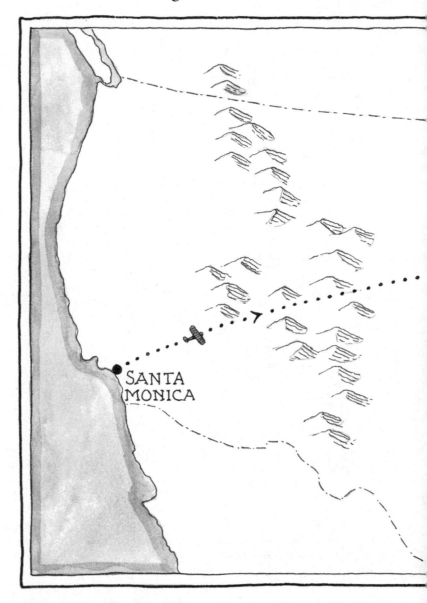

considered changing the flight path or making a male navigator go along in every plane.

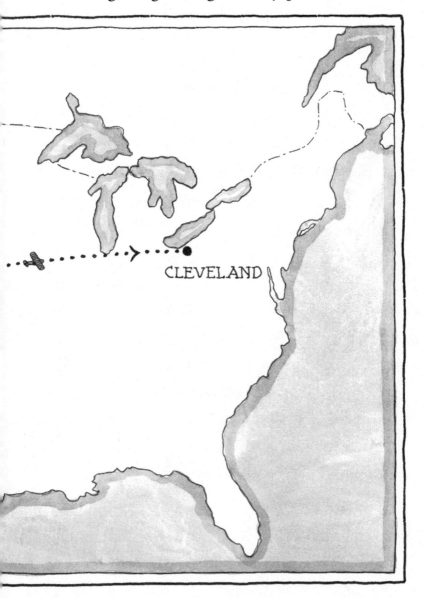

CLEVELAND

Map of the race route over the Rocky Mountains

Needless to say, Amelia was very angry. She and other women pilots had flown many hours alone. Amelia said she would not enter the race if she couldn't fly on her own. Because of Amelia and several other female pilots, the committee backed down. The women would fly the whole course by themselves.

On August 18, 1929, twenty thousand people

turned up in Santa Monica, California, for the start of the race. There were 19 pilots, including Amelia. Many people did not take the women seriously. Will Rogers, a famous writer at the time, called the race the "Powder Puff Derby." Still, by that Sunday afternoon all 19 planes were in the air and racing against the clock.

The race was to take eight days. But there were

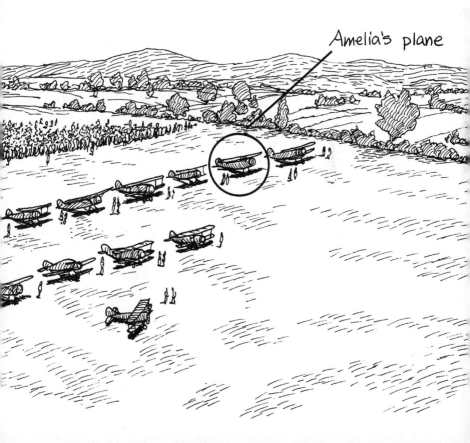

Amelia's plane

problems from the start. Planes broke down. Landing fields were not in good shape.

On the second day, Amelia's plane flipped over on landing. She wasn't hurt and she was able to fix her plane and keep racing.

But others weren't so lucky. Some planes went off course and crashed. One pilot died in the mountains of Arizona.

On August 25, the race was over. Only 11 of the 19 women finished. Amelia Earhart came in third. Even though she didn't win, Amelia learned a lot. She also got to know many of the best women pilots in the country.

After the race, many women pilots decided it was time to start their own group. On November 2, 1929, twenty-six women met in an airplane hangar in Long Island, New York. They wondered what to call themselves. Amelia suggested they name the club after the number of women who first joined. The other pilots liked the idea. Over the next several months the name changed from the Eighty-Sixes to the Ninety-Sevens. Finally, the Ninety-Nines was the name that stuck.

Amelia worked to get more women pilots to join. By the following summer, the Ninety-Nines had almost two hundred members. The group helped women pilots get jobs. The Ninety-Nines also had an office where careful records of women's aviation achievements could be kept. Amelia Earhart was elected the first president of the group.

Sometimes Amelia felt she didn't deserve all the praise that the public gave her. But she had truly earned the respect of the other women fliers. And it meant a lot to her.

Chapter 6
Amelia the Businesswoman

In the fall of 1929, the stock market crashed. Many people lost a lot of money. Many also lost their jobs. It was the start of the Great Depression. Amelia worried about her parents who had split up again. Her mother was living with Amelia's sister and husband. Amelia helped out by giving her mother some money every month. Her father was ill. So Amelia bought the log cabin in Los Angeles where he was living. Amelia felt a strong sense of duty to her parents.

THE GREAT DEPRESSION

It started on October 29, 1929. That was the day a lot of people lost a lot of money on the stock market. Since they had less money, people couldn't buy things. Businesses had to close. Millions of people lost their jobs. Soup kitchens were set up to feed people. The hungry waited for hours in long lines hoping to get a little free food.

The Great Depression dragged on for years. Mother Nature made things even worse. There was very little rain in the Great Plains during the 1930s. Farmland turned to dust. More families became homeless.

Under President Franklin Roosevelt, the government formed a plan to make things better. It was called the New Deal. Jobs were created. People began to make money again. By the end of the decade, the worst was over. But people who lived through the Great Depression would never forget the hard times.

Amelia had to keep earning money but that was not easy during the Depression. She still gave speeches but she had another job, too. Amelia helped start an airline on the East Coast. It was called The New York, Philadelphia and Washington Airway because it flew between those cities. Amelia's job was to convince people to fly on the airline.

It was difficult to run an airline in the early days. Only a few cities had airports. Once three planes arrived in Philadelphia at the same time. Some passengers had to change planes. Some people just got off to stretch their legs. But airline workers got confused. They put people on the wrong planes. Some were accidentally flown back to the city they had just left!

Another problem on the early flights was airsickness. It wasn't just the bumps. Fumes from the engine often came into the cabin. There also was

AVIATION INDUSTRY

Today traveling by plane seems as normal as taking a bus. But it wasn't always that way. In fact, your grandparents may not have stepped foot on an airplane until they were grown-ups!

At first airplanes primarily delivered mail, not people. But the many small companies that carried mail sometimes allowed passengers to travel as well. By the late 1920s, these smaller companies combined to form four larger airlines—TWA, United, Eastern, and American. They were known as the "Big Four" and were the first to schedule passenger-only flights. In 1923, the first nonstop flight to travel across the country carried passengers from New York to San Diego. It would be another thirty years before a passenger jet traveled nonstop between New York and London. By mid-century, the airline industry in the United States had truly taken off!

no air conditioning. Sometimes more than half of the passengers on a plane threw up. Still, more than fifteen hundred passengers flew on the tiny airline during the first ten days. Amelia was happy to report that almost half the tickets had been sold to women.

Besides working with the airline and taking care of her family, Amelia was still trying to set records. That was part of being Amelia Earhart, the celebrity. In the summer of 1930, Amelia set three new speed records. The fastest speed she recorded was 180 miles per hour. Today the average passenger jet flies at around 500 to 700 miles per hour.

Amelia was doing exactly what she had dreamed of doing. It was an exciting time. But then, in September of 1930, Amelia received bad news. Her father had cancer. He would not live much longer. Amelia flew out to see him in California. She stayed with her father for four

days. She took care of him and said her good-byes. During her return trip to New York, she got word that her father had died.

It was a very sad time for Amelia. She missed her father. She also was under a lot of pressure. She worked for an airline. She gave speeches all over the country. She raced her airplane and set records.

She took care of her family. Amelia was tired. She needed help. Amelia turned to her long-time manager, George Putnam.

George Putnam was divorced now and wanted to marry Amelia. Amelia had said no many times. But maybe marriage to George Putnam could be different. George was ten years older than Amelia. He already had two grown children. George wouldn't expect Amelia to stay at home. In fact, he wanted to help her become even more famous.

Amelia decided to take the risk.

On February 7, 1931, she and George Putnam were married.

Both bride and groom were in agreement on one important issue. Amelia would definitely keep her career.

And although she didn't plan it, she even got to keep her name. Although she officially became Amelia Earhart Putnam after her marriage, the press didn't like the change. They soon dropped the "Putnam" and called her Amelia Earhart—just as they always had.

Chapter 7
Pushing the Limits

By 1931, there were many changes in the world of flying. Slow, wood-framed airplanes had been replaced with faster all-metal models. The new planes had better instruments. Pilots could find their locations more easily and fly more safely.

The newer planes were bigger and carried more passengers. Slowly, the public was won over to airplane travel. After all, it took four hours to go to

Washington from New York by train. By plane the trip was only two and a half hours. In 1930, the first three flight attendants were hired by United Airlines. They were all nurses. They served meals and then took care of airsick passengers.

There were also more than 450 licensed female pilots in the United States. With more competition, it was getting harder to keep the public's interest. Amelia needed to do something different. She and George came up with a few ideas.

Amelia started flying something called an autogyro. It was almost like a helicopter. Amelia became the first person to go across the country and back in an autogyro. But the autogyro was hard to fly. Many pilots thought it wasn't safe. Soon Amelia went back to a regular airplane.

One January morning in 1932, Amelia was having breakfast with her husband. She put down the paper she was reading and asked, "Would you mind if I flew the Atlantic alone?"

No! George didn't mind at all. He wanted Amelia to become the first woman to fly solo across the Atlantic.

May 20, 1932, was the fifth anniversary of the Lindbergh flight. George Putnam thought that would be the perfect date for Amelia to take off. The press would love the connection.

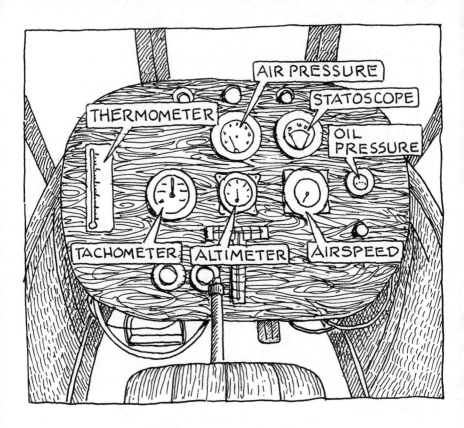

Amelia had new instruments, including three compasses, put in her plane. The weather over the Atlantic could be bad. She would depend on the new technology to help her find her way.

On the day of her flight, Amelia told reporters she was sure of her success. But before she climbed into her plane she quietly turned to a friend. "Do you think I can make it?" she asked. Even Amelia had her doubts.

Amelia took off from Harbour Grace airport in Newfoundland, Canada. Amelia didn't think the flight would be easy . . . and it wasn't. When she went too high, ice started to build on her wings. The ice made the plane heavy; it might crash. So she took the plane down low. But when she went too close to the water, her instruments didn't work. Without instruments, Amelia could get completely lost.

The hours went by slowly. Amelia struggled to find just the right altitude. She sipped chicken soup. Gasoline dripped down the back of her neck from the extra fuel tank. She struggled all night.

But when the sun came up Amelia spotted land. She set her airplane down in a cow pasture, "frightening all the cows." She was in Ireland. She had done it! Amelia was the first woman to fly solo across the Atlantic Ocean.

Congratulations poured in. Amelia was thirty-four years old. She was smart. She was brave . . . and she was a great-looking woman. The public loved her. When she returned to New York City, there was a parade down Broadway. Thousands of people lined the streets to cheer for Amelia.

The next day, Amelia flew to Washington, D.C., where President Herbert Hoover presented her with a medal.

Herbert Hoover and Amelia

Amelia was as famous as movie stars of the day, but her fame did not change her. She was still charming and somewhat shy. Even so, she liked that her opinions were now heard and respected.

Amelia became more active in politics. She joined the National Women's Party. Amelia thought women should be able to do the same things men did. For example, if a woman wanted to be a lawyer, then she should be able to do so. In a letter to the editor of a New York paper Amelia stated her case. "The right to earn a living belongs to all persons."

Amelia certainly took that message to heart. Now that she was so famous, she found many different ways to make money. Amelia was already known as one of the best-dressed women in America. This gave her husband an idea. George Putnam made some calls. Not long after, Macy's department store in New York made an announcement. A new line of women's clothing was going to be designed by—Amelia Earhart.

Amelia designed women's clothes for "active living." Amelia believed that clothes should fit the way a woman lived. She liked fabrics that didn't

Amelia Earhart Luggage

wrinkle. She also liked clothes that were easy to wash and didn't need special care.

Fashion designing took up a lot of her time. Amelia's photograph was in many magazines. She was always in demand. But flying was still Amelia's passion. Nothing else could match the adventure and challenge.

A group of Hawaiian businessmen had an idea. They asked Amelia to become the first person to fly solo from Honolulu to California. It would be a 2,500 mile nonstop trip over the Pacific Ocean.

On January 11, 1935, Amelia took off from Honolulu. Eighteen and a half hours later, she

landed in Oakland, California. She did it. It was another one for the record book.

Amelia always said she flew for the fun of it. But some people said she took too many risks.

Others didn't like George. He was constantly trying to make money from Amelia's name and fame.

Amelia was beginning to feel trapped. It was getting harder to set new records. Each time she had to fly farther and longer. Setting records took money. There was always new and better equipment to buy. However, there was one more flight she was determined to take. It would be the biggest challenge of all.

Chapter 8
The Final Flight

Amelia Earhart wanted to fly around the world. Although other pilots had circled the globe, she would fly close to the equator. This would make a longer and harder trip—29,000 miles.

A special plane was needed—a new Lockheed model called the Electra. The plane was large

enough to carry ten passengers. But Amelia had the seats removed. Extra fuel tanks were put in. This allowed the plane to fly up to three thousand miles before stopping to refuel.

The Electra had new radio equipment. Amelia would be able to communicate by voice and code. It also had two engines that made it more complicated to fly. Amelia had to train with different pilots to learn how to fly it. It would take months to prepare for the trip.

Amelia and George hired two navigators to fly with Amelia. They would help Amelia stay on course.

The flight path would go from east to west. Amelia would take off from California and head toward Hawaii. On March 17, 1937, the Electra left Oakland, California. Amelia and her two navigators arrived in Honolulu about 16 hours later. The first leg of the trip was a success.

Then Amelia had an accident.

As Amelia was taking off from Honolulu, the plane lurched out of control. The landing gear collapsed. A wing was torn open. Luckily, no one was hurt. But the $100,000 plane was badly damaged. It had to be shipped back to Lockheed on the

mainland. Almost two months went by before the plane was ready to fly again.

Because of the delay, one of the navigators could not continue the flight. That left only the other man—Fred Noonan.

There was also another change. Due to weather patterns, the flight path had to be reversed. Amelia would now fly from west to east. On May 21, Amelia left Oakland, California, and headed east to Miami, Florida. The whole world was watching.

The trip started off well. From Miami, Amelia flew to Puerto Rico. Then she flew along the east coast of South America to Venezuela, then on to Surinam and Brazil. The Electra was holding up well. But there was not much room to move around. Amelia communicated with Fred Noonan

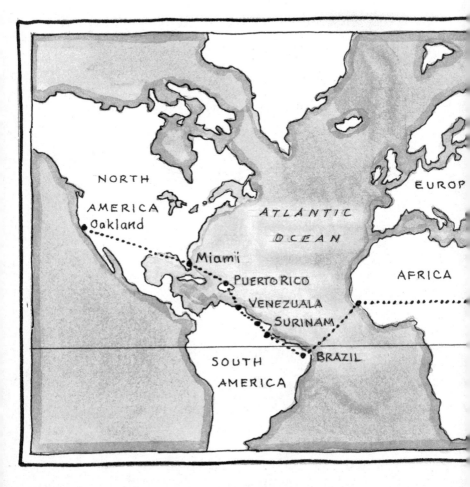

by passing notes on a fishing pole. It was better than climbing over the extra fuel tanks.

Amelia flew over forty hours and four thousand miles in the first week. And that was just the beginning. She flew over the Atlantic and crossed to Africa. Within three weeks she had flown twenty

Amelia's flight path of last trip

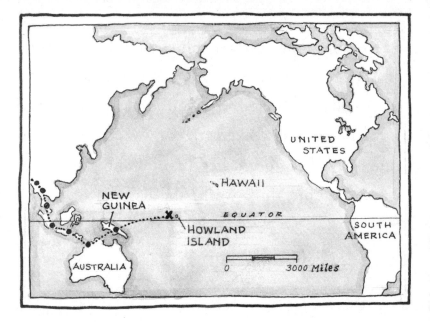

thousand miles in 135 hours. Amelia was getting tired. She would be glad when the long hours of flying were over.

By July 1, Amelia had reached New Guinea. From New Guinea she'd go to Howland Island and then to Honolulu, Hawaii. The next—and

last—stop would be Oakland, California. There were only 7,000 miles left on the 29,000 mile trip. Most of these last miles were over the Pacific Ocean.

On July 2, Amelia took off from New Guinea. The trip to Howland was to take about 19 hours. Howland was a tiny island in the Pacific. It was only two miles long and three quarters of a mile wide. It would be very hard to find. But it was the only place to land and refuel. Amelia had to depend on Fred Noonan to spot the tiny strip of sand.

To help Amelia and Fred, a U.S. Coast Guard ship was sent to Howland. The ship would be waiting at the island. It would send out a  signal to guide the Electra in for landing.

On July 2, Amelia took off from New Guinea. She had radio contact with New Guinea for the next seven hours. But then she went out of range. Amelia was supposed to reach Howland Island early the next morning. Throughout the night, the radiomen on the Coast Guard ship heard short messages from Amelia. But they could not tell how far out she was. The captain was worried. Amelia did not seem to hear their radio messages. And they couldn't get a fix on her when she called in to them.

At 7:42 A.M., the radiomen on the Coast Guard ship got a brief message. Amelia said, "We must be

on you but cannot see you and gas is running low. Been unable to reach you by radio." Again, the Coast Guard tried to respond. However, it seemed that Amelia could still not hear them. They tried to locate her plane. But her messages were not long enough to do it.

At 8:45 A.M., one more message came in from Amelia. The last thing she said was "We are running north and south." Amelia was frantically searching for Howland Island. But she never found it.

Right away a rescue mission was begun. More than four thousand men on ten ships searched the Pacific. Another 65 airplanes flew in to help search for Amelia and Fred.

So what happened? Did Amelia's plane crash into the Pacific Ocean? Or was she able to land on some remote island? Neither Fred Noonan nor Amelia Earhart were ever found or heard from again.

The mystery captured the public's imagination. For years after the plane's disappearance, "news" stories would pop up. Some said Amelia was a prisoner of war. Others said she was alive and well, living on a remote island. But no story was ever proven true.

Even today, people are still looking for Amelia's plane. An underwater robot submarine has scoured the Pacific Ocean floor where the Electra may have gone down. Search parties still occasionally hike through remote Pacific islands near Howland, hoping to find a clue in the overgrown jungles.

Who knows? Someday the remains of Amelia's plane may be found. Whether that happens or not, it doesn't change what Amelia Earhart did in her lifetime. She didn't just fly planes. She didn't just break records. She opened doors for women all over the world. She was a pioneer who said, "You can do anything you decide to do."

Timeline of Amelia's Life

1897	Amelia Earhart is born on July 24 in Atchison, KS.
1909	Amelia attends the Iowa State Fair and sees her first airplane
1916	Amelia enrolls in Ogontz School
1918	Amelia enters Columbia University in New York City
1920	Amelia moves to Los Angeles
1921	Amelia receives her pilot's license
1924	Amelia sells her plane, the *Canary*, and moves to Boston
1928	Amelia flies in the *Friendship* across the Atlantic
1929	On August 25, Amelia finishes third in the Women's Air Derby Amelia helps to start a new airline
1930	Amelia sets three new records for speed. Amelia's father dies
1931	Amelia marries George Putnam on February 7
1932	Amelia becomes the first woman to fly alone across the Atlantic
1935	Amelia becomes the first person to fly solo from the United States to Hawaii
1937	On June 1, Amelia embarks on her round-the-world journey On July 2, Amelia's plane is lost over the Pacific Ocean

Timeline of The World

Orville and Wilbur Wright fly first airplane at Kitty Hawk, NC —— 1903

Henry Ford develops the first Model T automobile —— 1908

World War I begins in Europe —— 1914

World War I ends —— 1918

19th Amendment gives women the right to vote —— 1920

Charles Lindbergh flies first successful solo non-stop flight from —— 1927
New York to Paris

Penicillin discovered by Alexander Fleming —— 1928

United States enters Depression after the stock market collapses —— 1929

Pluto discovered by astronomers —— 1930

Franklin Delano Roosevelt is elected president —— 1932

Dr. Seuss's first children's book is published —— 1937

BIBLIOGRAPHY

Rich, Doris. **Amelia Earhart: A Biography.** The Smithsonian Institution Press; Washington and London, 1989.

Butler, Susan. **East to the Dawn: The Life of Amelia Earhart.** Da Capo Press, Inc., New York, 1999.

Sloate, Susan. **Amelia Earhart: Challenging the Skies.** Fawcett Columbine (Ballantine Books), New York, 1990.

Szabo, et al. **Sky Pioneer: A Photobiography of Amelia Earhart.** National Geographic Press, Washington, 1997.